A Staffordshire W

Living in the workhouse of Nev

By Gladys Dinnacombe

ISBN: 978-1-326-92570-3

Also by Gladys Dinnacombe

Poetry and Prose
Sacred Journey—Sacred Earth
So You Want to be a Druid? - First steps on the path
The World Around Me – A Modern Druid Philosophy
So You Still Want to be a Druid – Further steps on the Path
A Long and Winding Road – The Life and Travels of a Spiritual Wanderer
Twiglets, Twigs and Branches – Growing a family tree

Acknowledgements

Thank you to the following:

Helen Burton, Keele Special Collections – Warrilow Collection, Keele University Library, Keele Staffordshire

Staffordshire Record Office, Stafford

Stoke Archives, Hanley, Stoke-on-Trent, Staffs.

Staffordshire Arts and Museums Service

Simon Hall for the publishing stuff and for encouragement

Melanie Whitehead for proof reading and encouragement

Brampton Museum for the photographs on pages 23 and 24

Chapter 1

The Newcastle-under-Lyme Poor Law Union did not formally come into being until 3rd April 1838 so what help was there for the poor before that date. Before then, the borough had tried to avoid the need for poor rates. Around 1657 a malt mill was erected and this was to provide maintenance for the poor. The income from the leasing of the mill was meant to be sufficient to provide for the poor but if there was a shortfall then the poor were to receive £12 per year out of the toll of corn which was ground at the mill. Other new sources of income were found as needed. When the malt mill was sold in 1796 the money raised went to the poor.

From 1622 overseers of the poor were appointed by the borough. The post of overseer of the poor continued until 1925 when it was abolished.

The type of relief for the poor included weekly or occasional payments of money, rent payments, medical attention and grants for apprenticeships. During the 17th century those in receipt of poor relief were made to wear red badges in the shape of a castle. This was later discontinued. But if the poor were given clothing at certain times there were rules about the colour of the clothing. In 1742 males had green clothing and females had yellow clothing. This must have been very humiliating for them.

In 1731 houses in the Higherland area were converted into a workhouse where the poor were also employed. By 1776 there was room for forty persons.

There were also Almshouse in the town, provided by the Duke of Sutherland for women, mainly aged around 60 and 70 who may also have been incapacitated. These almshouses were considered by the Duke to be a charity not a workhouse.

There is much more information in the Victoria County History if you wish to know more.

Chapter 2

When the Newcastle under Lyme Poor Law Union came into being in 1838, a Board of Guardians was elected. There were eighteen of these representing the nine parishes of the Union. Some parishes had more than one Guardian. These parishes were Audley, with three Guardians; Balterley, Betley with two Guardians; Chapel Chorlton. Keele. with two Guardians, Maer, Newcastle with six Guardians and Whitmore.

At the first meeting of the Guardians in early April 1838, the Guardians elected were as follows;

Mr Jesse Prime, George Cooper, Joseph Cliff, W. U. Lester, F. Stanier and R. Broughton for Newcastle; R. E. Heathcote, Esq. , John Booth and W. Robotham for Audley; Rev. J. W. Daltry and Mr. R. Hill for Madeley; Rev. H. Purton for Betley; Mr. Glover for Balterley; Mr. S. Peake and S. Worthington for Keele; Capt. R. Mainwaring for Whitmore; Rev. J. A. Wedgwood for Maer and Mr. Joseph Stanley for Chapel Chorlton. Capt. Mainwaring was appointed Chairman.

The Guardians agreed to meet every Monday at 10 o'clock to start with as there was a great deal of business to discuss. Various officers were appointed such as the Vice Chairman and Treasurer. They also decided to have only one relieving officer and salaries for this and for a Clerk were also discussed. Mr. Tilsley was appointed as Relieving Officer at at a salary of £105 per year.

At the second meeting of the Guardians a Clerk was appointed, Mr. Samuel Harding. Mr. Harding had been the Registrar of

Births, etc and Clerk to the Newcastle Vestry and had several years of experience.

At the time of this meeting there was a small workhouse in Newcastle and one in Audley as well as three more elsewhere in the area. But there was a need for a larger workhouse and this committee of Guardians resolved to have a new workhouse which would accommodate three hundred upwards inmates. The cost would be borrowed from the government and repaid over twenty years. A new Registrar was also appointed. The previous Governor of the workhouse, Mr. Whittaker was also mentioned.

At the following meeting, tenders for the erection of the new workhouse were received and Mr. John Shaw of Madeley was given the contract. The plans were those of Messrs. Scott and Moffatt and included a set of rooms for married couples. At this same meeting Miss Sarah Hand was appointed schoolmistress at the Newcastle workhouse and Mr. G Fox was reappointed as Master of Newcastle workhouse and given a salary rise of ten shillings.

The new workhouse was built in 1838/9 on Keele Road in Newcastle. It cost £6000 and could house three hundred and fifty inmates. There was separate accommodation for males and females, an infirmary, laundry, workshop and accommodation for the Master at the workhouse.

An interesting advertisement in December 1838 was for persons willing to contract for the supply of one of any of the articles listed and tenders with samples where appropriate were to be sent to the Clerk to the Guardians. The items included cheese per cwt., peas per bushel, rice per cwt., oatmeal per bad of twenty pounds, soap per cwt., salt, salt butter, vinegar, tea, coffee, sugar, treacle, pepper, soda, starch, blue, blacklead and candles. Also listed was bread, of the best seconds flour, per stone and baked upon the over bottom. Meat, beef, rounds, bosoms, stickings and suet were per pound and also mutton. The bread and meat was to be delivered once a week to the workhouse of Newcastle and Audley.

In 1841 the Master of the Workhouse was George Fox. He was 35 (bearing in mind rounded up ages on the census) and his wife Eliza, also 35 was the Matron. The other staff comprised a schoolmistress, a porter and a female servant. There were fifty five male inmates and sixty five female inmates. Of these more than fifty were children under twelve years of age.

George Fox was actually 29 or 30 not 35 after checking the following census. He was still Master of the Workhouse in 1861. So what were the duties of the Master and what qualifications were needed?

First of all the Master had to be over the age of twenty one and be able to keep the accounts as he needed enough education to do this. He also had to have a strong will and know how to be firm in his dealings with others. But he was also expected to be considerate and gentle, tolerant, never using profane language or losing his temper.

The duties of the Master were many. Not only was the paperwork for admission and the registration of births and deaths and the various reports to the Guardians, but daily roll-calls, prayers before meals and the checking of inmates was also done. There were many rules to enforce and the buildings had to be kept clean and in good repair. The Master also dealt with the male inmates, ensuring their cleanliness and that they were properly clothed. If the Master was married then his wife acted as the Matron overseeing the female inmates.

So what kind of people were the Master and Matron? I have not been able to find out much about the background of George Fox and his wife. But there were two kinds of Workhouse Masters. We read about the bad ones and their cruelty but they could not all have been bad and I wonder what kind of Master George Fox was. As the workhouse expanded, there would be more work to do and the job could be seen as very stressful.

In 1841 there was also a schoolmistress. She would instruct both boys and girls for at least three hours every day. They would learn to read and write as well as do basic arithmetic, religion and anything else that might help them to find work later. The schoolmistress was also in charge of keeping the children clean and tidy as well as orderly.

Two other people were employed at the Workhouse in 1841, one was a female servant and the other a porter. According to an advertisement in the Staffordshire Advertiser of 25 February 1841, the porter would receive £15 per annum with reasonable use of the provisions consumed in the house. A tailor or shoemaker was preferred.

In an interesting document date 3 March 1841 concerning the death of a pauper James Smith at the Newcastle Workhouse, the Coroner stated that the pauper died through want of the common necessities of life and that blame is attributed to the officers of the workhouse for not having given more prompt relief and that the vagrant ward was damp and unwholesome. James Smith was only 35 years of age. This report does give some insight into how George Fox behaved as Master of the Workhouse. (Ref MH12/11363/212)

I found two documents listing deaths in the Newcastle Workhouse during 1839 and 1840. There were eighteen deaths in 1839, the youngest an infant and the oldest sixty four. Six were due to consumption, and five due to inflammation of the chest and/or lungs. In 1840 there were thirty deaths, the youngest again an infant and the oldest aged eighty five. Nineteen of the deaths were young children, six of these due to measles.

Chapter 3

In the years between 1841 and 1850 there are several interesting documents available. The first one which is heavily annotated and dated 1845 (MH12/11363/178) goes into great detail about the admission, classification, discipline and diet of paupers as well as details of the officers and their duties. (discussed elsewhere)

Paupers were classified as follows:
- men infirm through age or other causes;
- able bodied men and youths over thirteen;
- boys aged seven and under thirteen;
- women infirm through age or other causes;
- able bodied women and girls over the age of sixteen;
- girls over the age of seven and under sixteen;
- children under seven.

The diet sheets showed that men had more food than women. For breakfast there was bread and milk porridge. Men had seven ounces of bread and women five ounces. Dinner consisted of cooked meat and potatoes, six ounces of meat for men and five ounces for women. Some days there was rice, eighteen ounces but no meat. Supper consisted of bread and cheeses or broth. It was a diet that kept you alive but not much else as far as I can see.

Another document in 1846 gave details of vaccinations which I assume were for smallpox. Of those given, most of them seemed to work although some did fail. There was a cholera epidemic in 1848/9 but I have few details of this although it was mentioned in an inspection report of 1847

(MH12/11364/177) The report stated that the provision for the sick and infectious was inadequate due to the great influx of Irish, many of whom were suffering from fever. There were nine cases in the workhouse. The vagrants rooms were being used for the fever cases. The relieving officer was told that he must live in town in order to do his job properly. Another inspection report in 1849 noted the presence of cholera in the workhouse and that there had been two hundred deaths in Newcastle borough.

The Guardians were elected annually and by law had to be ratepayers who occupied property for which the rates were at least £25 per year. The Guardians were elected by the rate payers of the parish which the Guardians represented. Magistrates were often ex officio members of the Board of Guardians.

A report in the Staffordshire Advertiser of 14 April 1855 states that the only contest in the election of the Guardians of the Poor was in the parish of Newcastle where twelve persons were nominated. It turned out that those who had been Guardians the previous year were re-elected. These were Mr. J. D. Mort by 587 votes; Mr. J. Lamb by 563 votes; Mr. T. Turner by 560 votes; Mr. H. Farr by 462 votes; Mr. C. Lawton by 450 votes and the Rev. W. Chambers by 416 votes.

The Staffordshire Sentinel, Birmingham, Wolverhampton and Midland Adviser of 31 March 1855 gives more details of some of the nominees. Mr. John Lamb of Marsh Terrace was a paper manufacturer, Mr. John D. Mort of Keele Road was a newspaper proprietor; Mr. Thomas Turner of High Street was a druggist; Mr. Charles Lawton also of Marsh Terrace was a gas contractor; Mr. Henry Farr of Marsh, was a coachmaker; Mr.

George Harrison of High Street was a carver and gilder; Mr. Thomas Coleman of High Street was a pawnbroker and Mr. William Hargreaves also of High Street was a grocer. There were two more grocers, Mr Thomas Highfield and Mr. John Bull while Mr William Palk of High Street was a fancy ware dealer.

In 1851 the Master of the workhouse was still George Fox and his wife Eliza was still the Matron. There are now more members of staff. The schoolmistress has been joined by a schoolmaster. As well as the Porter there is now a baker and a sick nurse as well as a female servant. There are 62 male inmates and 60 female inmates. Of these 51 are children aged 12 and under, hence the need for another schoolteacher. It is possible that the nurse joined the staff during the cholera epidemic and then stayed on.

Schoolmaster and schoolmistresses were subject to a grading scale in four parts. The first part was called Permission, the next Probation, the third Competency and the final stage Efficiency. By the time the Efficiency grade was reached the master or mistress should have attained good biblical knowledge, English Grammar, composition, etymology, decimal arithmetic, geography of the British Empire especially, outlines of English history and be able to organise and manage a school. They were inspected regularly.

Documents from 1854 and 1855 award a certificate of Efficiency to Thomas Eli Bennet, late schoolmaster of the Newcastle under Lyme workhouse and to Henry Harrison a certificate of Efficiency while Mary Lodge received a certificate of Permission. When Henry Harrison was appointed in 1855 his annual salary was £30 and he was provided with rations and other allowances assigned by the guardians. The schoolmaster in 1855 was Mr. H. Williamson who resigned because of ill-health. Mr. Henry Harrison was appointed in his place. Henry Harrison was 23, unmarried and lived previously in Hull where he was a pupil teacher for five years and then as a schoolmaster in Lexden and Winstree Union in Essex where he had resigned in consequence of punishing a boy more severely than approved of.

The duties of a sick nurse are fairly obvious but as well as caring for the sick and those lying-in, arrangements in the wards had to be checked for any defects and a light had to be kept lit during the night. The nurse was either single or widowed with no dependants

There are some interesting stories in the newspapers about the workhouse inmates. In January 1851, there is a report about the boys in the workhouse who had been occupied during the year in gardening. They had cultivated two acres of land and the crops which were grown and sold provided a profit of over £27. There were thirteen boys involved most of them aged twelve and under.

In 1852, the newspaper reported the death of a five year old boy who had wandered into a room with a guarded open fire and had got too close and set his clothes on fire. Sadly he died a few hours later.

A burglary at the workhouses was recorded in 1853 where £4 worth of copper had been taken and drawers and cupboards ransacked.

One   of   the   most   interesting   set   of   documents

(MH12/11365/104, 105, 109 and 116) from 1853 document the inquest into the death of Samuel Hassall, an inmate at the workhouse. There was a lot of controversy over evidence given at the inquest and an inquiry was conducted. The coroners verdict was that Samuel Hassall had died from exhaustion caused by a burst abscess. The jury believed that considerable blame for his death was attached to the Master and Matron for not acting sooner. The inquiry led by Andrew Doyle, Poor Law Inspector exonerated the Master and Matron. Reading all the evidence given, it is fairly obvious that some people were lying. It is not the first case involving George Fox Master of the workhouse. I gave details earlier of a case in 1841.

A document of 1855 detailing a letter from the Medical Office of Newcastle under Lyme Union Workhouse to the Poor Law Board states that the Clerk to the Union and the Master of the workhouse had requested him not to enter patients admitted into the workhouse Infirmary on Saturdays, on the sick list for that day, as by doing so it made difficulties for the Master in making his book. This feels like Mr. Fox was more interested in his paperwork than in those under his care.

The workhouse was inspected regularly and especially those considered to be lunatics or idiots. One such inspection report (MH12/11365/247) states that the idiotic inmates were free from excitement, clean in person, well clad and generally usefully occupied and in good bodily health. But the Inspector recommended that the practice of placing two idiotic male inmates in the same bed should be discontinued and that the epileptics should be dressed in woollen clothing.

In 1856, details of accommodation showing sizes of rooms and details of the class of inmates accommodated can be found in a document (MH12/11365/268). Some rooms were only occupied by day while others were occupied by both day and night. The men's day room was 26 feet 3 inches long, 16 feet 6 inches wide and 9 feet 9 inches in height. The old men's day room was slightly shorter but the same width and height. The girls day room was larger than that of the boys, 26 feet 6 inches compared to 16 feet 6 inches. The rooms used at night and also by day were generally smaller while those used by night only were much larger being 49 feet 9 inches long. There was a small room for aged couples. There were twenty rooms in total with the number of people who could be accommodated being 218.

But what of those living in the workhouse? There were many elderly widowed men, a lot of children but few families. I found Jane Yearsley, 55, born in Audley and stating she was widowed, with Thomas, her son aged 15 and born in Wolstanton. In 1841 the family had been living in Chesterton Village. Jane was head of the family and a washerwoman. There were several children, Abel, aged 13, Harriet, 10; Joseph, 8; Thomas. 5 and Elizabeth, 2. So what happened to the other children? Elizabeth died in 1843 aged 4 and was buried in St. Giles churchyard. Joseph may have died in 1839 but I have not confirmed this. Abel and Harriet are not found on the 1851 census.

There were also two brothers, John Keeling aged 13 and Thomas aged 10, both born in Newcastle. In 1841, John and Thomas can be found living in Lower Street with their parents and other siblings. Father John was aged 40, mother Sarah the same age and siblings James, 12; Elizabeth,10; Sarah 8, Johns age given as 3 and Thomas's as 6 months. John, the father, had married Sarah Cope on 12 November 1826 at St. Nicholas,

Fulford. John had been born on 16th June 1801 and christened on 24th July at St. Giles, Newcastle. His father was called Thomas. John did not die until 1857 and was buried on 1st March at St. George, Newcastle. His wife Sarah died in 1843 and was buried on 22nd March. John could have been ill before his death and this may be the reason the two children were in the workhouse. Of the other children, James married Ann Haynes in 1857 and they had a daughter Sarah. I have found nothing about the other children. John left the workhouse and married Ann Shufflebotham in 1863. In 1871 they lived in Marsh Terrace with two children, Elizabeth and Emma and Ann's mother Elizabeth Shufflebotham. By 1881 they had moved to Hassall Street and had two more children. In 1891 John is working as a refreshment house keeper at Hope Cottage, Broad Street, Newcastle. So his life had improved greatly after leaving the workhouse.

One last word about the workhouse here. After an inspection on 24th September 1857, Andrew Doyle, Esq., wrote 'I have this day inspected this workhouse which I have found in its usual satisfactory state.'

Chapter 4

The 1861 census shows that George Fox and his wife Eliza are still Master and Matron of the workhouse. There is still a schoolmaster and schoolmistress, as well as a nurse and a female servant. However the porter is also the baker. Of the inmates, sixty are male and sixty female. Of these twenty nine are children aged twelve and under.

Looking at and researching the family history of some of the inmates I found some interesting stories. Elizabeth Ashley, unmarried, age 61 and born in Audley is with her daughter Hannah aged 25. When looking for them in previous censuses, 1851 and 1841, I saw that they were both in the workhouse at that time. Elizabeth died in 1863 and Hannah in 1876. I hope that they had not been in the workhouse for the whole of that time.

A group of children all with the same name intrigued me. They were John Clark, aged 13, Thomas Clark aged 11, James aged 8 and Mark aged 6. John and Thomas were definitely brothers and can be found on the census of 1851 at Holborn, Newcastle with their parents Myles Clark and Catherine Clark. There are siblings too, Ann aged 14, Mary aged 10, Bridget aged 7 and Anthony aged 5. The father Miles was a fruit dealer, born in Ireland and died in 1860. So where were Catherine and the other children in 1861? Mary had married Joseph Hammersley in 1861 and they were living in Stoke on Trent. Anthony was a lodger elsewhere but I can find no trace of the others at this point in time. The other two children in the workhouse with the surname Clark are not the same family as far as I know.

Also in the workhouse was a father George Lane with his two daughters, Ann aged 12 and Mary aged 10. George was born in Uttoxeter so was easy to find on the previous census, where he was an innkeeper in Newcastle and living with his wife Elizabeth, daughter Ann aged 2 and a son George aged 4. In 1861, his wife Elizabeth appears on the census living with cousins in Leigh, Lancashire. George is possibly working in Worcestershire as an agricultural labourer.

Newspapers in this decade give more information about the workhouse, sometimes more than found in documents held by the National Archives. One of the interesting newspaper reports of 1861 concerns a young woman named Maria Lea, who was discharged from the Newcastle workhouse six weeks previously on the grounds she was not destitute, having received money and the medical officer, Dr. Hallam, said she was not likely to be confined for sometimes. The young woman, then went to the relieving officer for Stoke telling him she had been turned out of the Newcastle workhouse, was destitute and near her confinement. She was sent to the Stoke workhouse and the Newcastle Guardians contacted where an inquiry was held. The Clerk to the Guardians stated that Maria Lea was not destitute as she had spare clothes which she could have pledged and that she had done this earlier and had 21shillings in money which she then spent on clothes for herself and nothing for the coming baby. Maria Lea was not confined for another ten weeks. This case caused a great deal of unpleasantness for the Guardians of both workhouses.

A report in the Staffordshire Advertiser of 27 December 1862 states that the inmates of Newcastle Union workhouse had a very cheerful Christmas Day. Their dinner consisted of capital beef and pudding served on a 'most liberal scale' and was accompanied by a proper proportion of brown stout. Tobacco was given to those who loved a pipe and the entire day was spent in repose or relaxation. There were sweets for the children. At this time there were 144 inmates compared to 131 the previous year.

The 10 January 1863 edition of the Staffordshire Advertiser had an advertisement for the appointment of a Medical Officer for the Union workhouse in Newcastle and for the parishes of Newcastle, Keele and Madeley. The salary would be £70 per annum (£30 for the workhouse and £40 for the district) with the addition so extra medical fees according to the scale allowed by the Poor Law Board.

All seems quiet for some years as the next newspaper reports I have, deal with reports of fortnightly meetings and give details of contracts made for food, clothing, etc. The interesting details for me were that for the week ending 2 March 1867 there were 106 inmates, 366 receiving outdoor relief and in the following week there were 109 inmates and 358 receiving outdoor relief which consisted of money, or in kind. This shows how the number of inmates fluctuated week by week and also those needing help out door, as it was called, also fluctuated week by week. Later in the year, the Staffordshire Sentinel of 23 November 1867 reported the number of inmates as 106 and those receiving outdoor relief 398. This report also stated the unexpected death of the Master, George Fox on the previous Sunday.

In 1868, proposed new infectious wards were planned following a visit from Andrew Doyle, the Poor Law Inspector. Also in 1868, a spring cart, a set of harness, a hand hearse on springs and two gig wheels were to be sold by tender for the workhouse.

Another report of 2nd January 1869 gives details of numbers of inmates. For week ending 19th December there were 131 inmates, 15 were admitted and 10 discharged bringing the total to 138. Out door relief was given to 485. For the week ending 26 December the number of inmates was 138, 3 were admitted and none discharged so the total was 141. 473 received out door relief. A new Years concert was given to the inmates and some other invited people from the town.

I always wondered what happened to the children in the workhouse and another search at the National Archives brought to light information about some of the child inmates. The first of these is Elizabeth Joynson mentioned previously in a report from 1860 on insane persons, lunatics and idiots. On the 1861 census it can be seen that Elizabeth is deaf and dumb. By 1862 she had been elected a pupil at the Manchester school for the deaf and dumb if the Guardians provided her clothing and 2 shillings per week for her maintenance.. If this was done she could go to the school (MH12011367/48). They obviously complied as in a letter of 1865 (MH12/11367/308) it is stated that she has spent three years at the school but that the Guardians considered it important that she finish her education and stayed there so payments would be continued.

There are several letters concerning apprenticeships and the provision of clothing. Even if the provision of clothing was not granted there is information about the apprenticeship. The first of these in March 1867(MH12/11367/440 and 441) is for approval of money for clothing for William Henry Bayley being an apprentice to Henry Birtles, blacksmith of Audley. It is not clear whether this was approved.

The next one in April 1867 (MH11367/453) regards Samuel Barlow, aged 14 who has been in the workhouse since being deserted by his mother Amelia in infancy. The letter does not state who he is apprenticed to but that he gets board and lodging and 1 shilling per week for the first year. Amelia, Samael's mother was an inmate in the workhouse in 1851.

The next letter also dated April 1867 (MH12/ 11367/451) and concerns the apprenticeship of W. H. Bailey aged 15, son of John Bailey and Eliza Bailey. His father had deserted the family in 1855 and since that time the family had been in the workhouse. I would think that this is the William Henry Bayley mentioned above and if so the money for the clothing was approved.

In June 1867, a payment of £2.10s was given to Elizabeth Hancock for clothing on her leaving the workhouse. It was believed she would receive some wages for her service from her intended master. Later in the year, George Fox, the Master of the workhouse died suddenly which meant that his wife Eliza had to resign her post but she stayed on until another Master was appointed. It was hoped that this would occur on 16th December.

The following year 1868, more apprenticeships are noted as well as some inmates leaving the workhouse having obtained work. It seems that a clothing allowance of up to £2 was awarded in these cases. Hannah Billings, 19 left the workhouse to take a position in service with William Evans. (MH12/11202/89). Elizabeth Conway, 13, an orphan entered into the service of John Astbury. She would get board and lodging and 1 shilling per week for the first year of service

(MH12/11368/12 and 16). Charles Ward, 12, an orphan had been in the workhouse for eleven years. He was to work for Thomas Sherratt, a grocer of Bridge Street who would maintain and clothe him for two years. He would also pay for any schooling and provide occasional pocket money. (MH12/113681/157 and 161). Thomas Sherratt was well known and had previously taken boys from the workhouse who had done very well.

There are two more for 1869. Moses Brookes, 15, an orphan had been in the workhouse for nine years. He was apprenticed to George Harding, shoemaker of Albert Street, Tunstall. In November 1869, Martha Smith, 13, an orphan had been in the workhouse for eight years. Her proposed master was Thomas Edge, House of Haberdashers, Newcastle. As Martha was under the age of 14, the Board needed to check that she was fit (MH12/11368/235).

In 1870 the trend of finding employment for the children of the workhouse continued. Ann Lowndes, 13, an orphan, was to be hired for twelve months by George Barlow, farmer of Whitmore, who would provide her with maintenance, clothing and 1 shilling per week. Jane Joynson, 13, an illegitimate girl who had been born in the workhouse was to be hired for twelve months by Samuel Berks, a farmer of Knowl Bank, Audley. He would provide her with maintenance, clothing and 1 shilling per week. Jane was also given two suits of clothing on leaving the workhouse (MH12/11368/289).

In December 1870, George Rhodes, 14, who father was dead and his mother in the workhouse, was to be in the service of Daniel Proctor, blacksmith at Keele for one year. (MH12/11368/382). He would receive clothes and 1 shilling per week. On leaving the workhouse, he too received two suits of clothing worth £3.

But earlier in the year, in June, there had been allegations of cruelty by the Master of the workhouse, Mr. Cartwright by a 12 year old boy who had been caned on his back and hands and also boxed around the ears, the marks on his hands still showing after three weeks although he had been able to play cricket. It was decided that the cruelty charge was a 'cooked' one (MH12/11368/314). But the Staffordshire Advertiser report shows disagreement about whether the punishment was too severe and also infers that some members of the staff were silent as they did not want to lose their jobs.

Newcastle Workhouse

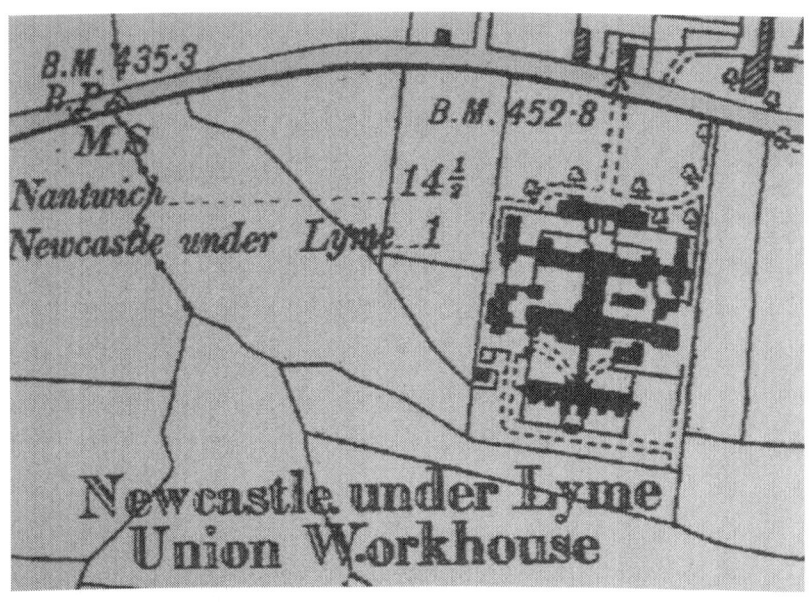

Map showing the workhouse

Workhouse plan

Keele Road staff of the workhouse 1920-30

Chapter 5

While searching for workhouse records I came upon a Poor Law Board Return of July 1861 listing all who had been inmates of the workhouse during a continuous period of five years. Those listed include two I mentioned earlier who I had found on the 1841, 1851, and 1861 census. According to this Poor Law Board Return they had been in the workhouse for twenty two years as they were of weak mind and unable to maintain themselves. There were ten others names on this return. James Johnson also of weak mind had been in the workhouse for seventeen years. On the 1861 census return he was aged thirty seven and had worked as a labourer. He was born in Alsagers Bank. There were three others of weak mind and unable to maintain themselves. Sarah Meadon who on the census of 1861 was aged forty two and had been in the workhouse for eight years; Sarah Dobson who was sixty in 1861 and had been in the workhouse for seven years; and Ann Harding who is in both the 1851 and 1861 censuses aged twenty six and thirty six respectively but who had spent six years continuously in the workhouse.

Elizabeth Pepper who was infirm from age had spent twenty years in the workhouse being in the 1841 and 1851 census aged fifty nine in 1851. Also aged and infirm was Sarah Cooper who was aged sixty in 1861 and had spent five years in the workhouse. John Rowe was also aged and infirm. He was aged seventy seven and a widower in 1861 and had also been in the workhouse for five years.

Ann Key, a widow and aged sixty six in 1861 suffered from asthma and had been in the workhouse for six years. Joseph

Wakelin suffered from fits and in 1851 was aged fifty six and widowed. He had been in the workhouse for seventeen years. The last name in the list, William Watson was also widowed and aged sixty one in 1851. The return states he was ruptured and had been in the workhouse for the years.

Two other reports of 1849 (MH12 11364-297) and 1852 (MH12-11365-86) also name those considered to be idiots, insane or of a weak mind. Some of the names are the same as those in the 1861 report while some are not on that report possibly because they had died by then, had also been in the workhouse for a large number of years. Two people named in all three reports are Elizabeth Ashley and Hannah Ashley. In 1849 they are described as idiotic but in the later reports they are of weak mind. In 1861 they had been in the workhouse for twenty two years. Elizabeth died in 1863 and was buried on 25 October at St. George, Newcastle. Hannah died in 1876.

Sarah Meadon appears on the 1852 report and also on that of 1861 where it is stated that she had been in the workhouse for eight years. She is in the workhouse on both the 1871 and 1881 censuses and died in 1886. Sarah was christened on 12 April 1818 in Newcastle and her parents were William and Mary. They had married in 1799 and had at least three children, Ann, Sarah and Henry born in 1876. In 1851, Mary who had married John Stockton in 1827 after the death of William, was again widowed. Living with her in Lower Street Newcastle were Sarah, Ann, Henry widowed with children William aged fifteen, John aged thirteen, Henry aged five and Kate aged three. In 1841 Henry had been living with his wife Ann and William and John in Gop Row. So why did Sarah end up in the workhouse? Mary her mother died in 1857, Henry died in either 1851 or. 1857, William died in 1855 and Kate in 1853.

John is lodging elsewhere in 1861 and Sarah and her sister Ann are both in the workhouse. Ann died in 1870 and Sarah in 1886.

Sarah Dobson named in the 1861 report as having a weak mind and resident in the workhouse for seven years is not mentioned in the earlier reports as she does not seem to have moved into the workhouse until around 1855. She was born in 1891 and in 1851 she is living with her parents Richard aged eighty and Jane aged seventy five. They both died in 1853. There must have been some kind of epidemic around that time asif it is also when many of Sarah Meadon's family died. Sarah Dobson lived in the workhouse until her death in 1871.

After the Master George Fox died in 1867, a new Master, George Cartwright was appointed and his wife Catherine was appointed Matron. They were both aged 33 in 1871 and stated they were born in Leicester. There was only a schoolmistress on the day of the census but that doesn't mean there wasn't one. There was a cook, a nurse and a man who was both porter and baker. There were sixty one male inmates and fifty five females and of these thirty seven were children twelve years and under.

Two of the inmates immediately caught my eye. These were Elizabeth Joynson now 19 and James's Joynson aged sixteen. Elizabeth had spent several years at the Manchester school for the deaf and dumb being supported by the Guardians of the Newcastle workhouse. But despite their efforts she was still without work. James Joynson was also deaf and dumb and was in the workhouse in 1861. It is likely that they were brother and sister. Sadly Elizabeth died in 1883.

In 1870/1 there seems to be a lot of changing of schoolmasters and schoolmistresses. In June 1870 we had James M. Willdig acquiring his Efficiency 2nd division certificate while his wife (we assume) Mary Willdig was not recommended for any certificates. (MH12/11368/273). By March 1871 the schoolmistress Margaret Copeland was recommended for her Competency 3rd division certificate. (MH12/11368/393) A schoolteacher could earn £30 per annum if certified or prepared to become certified.

In April 1871 there is an apprenticeship proposal for Peter Hobley, fourteen years nine months old. He was to be bound for six years to Samuel Gorman, a baker of Newcastle under Lyme. He would receive clothing, maintenance and one shilling per week from age seventeen and two shillings and sixpence per week for the years of the term. He would receive two suits of clothing worth £3 5shillings when he left the workhouse.

The details of fortnightly meetings of the Board of Guardians seem to have been published in the local newspapers but I have not found them all. However they do give an insight into the fluctuation of the number of inmates as well as other information. The workhouse returns, that is the number of admission and discharges plus the total number of inmates were dated to the end of each week. This of course was a job for the Master of the workhouse.

Chapter 6

1871 brought a change. The Local Government Board took over from the Poor Law Board but the Guardians kept their responsibility. Vagrants were also affected (see later pages).

In the Staffordshire Advertiser of 16th November 1872, the returns showed 116 inmates against 105 on the same date the previous year. Out-relief was given to 558 against 632 the previous year. A recent inspection brought to the attention of the Guardians the arrangements for vagrants which were very deficient. There was no bath or disinfecting stove. A separate infectious hospital was also needed. According to the Master, Mr. Cartwright, at this time an average of 27 vagrants a week needed workhouse accommodation. The vagrancy problem continued throughout 1873 until June when the Guardians were threatened with enforcement of the order. The vagrants were detained until 11 a.m. and this worked well. There was also a small epidemic of smallpox in 1873 but this appeared to be dying out.

There was also a discordant note in May 1873 concerning the payment of expenses for candidates for the posts of Master and Matron of the workhouse, some of whom had travelled a long way. The Board of Guardians thought that the previous Board should pay (out of their own pockets) as it was they who had caused the candidates to be sent for. By June 1873 smallpox was again on the increase and the sanitary conditions in the villages concerned, of the parish were described as very defective

Mr T Edwards was appointed Master of the workhouse in June

1873. Scarlet fever, diptheria and measles were also prevalent at this time. While the sanitation problems in the outlying villages continued to be a problem through out the year.

I have only seen two reports of the Board of Guardians for the year of 1874 and both of these were dated September. Was it that the reports were not published, or the newspaper unable to be preserved and scanned? One of the reports is from the Board of Guardians in Stoke. Pool Dam, situated in Newcastle but included in the parish of Stoke for poor rate purposes, was going to be annexed to the Newcastle Guardians but they also wanted The Cloughs which was situated in Seabridge. There was going to be an inquiry into these proposals.

By 24th September 1874, this proposal was ready to be confirmed by Parliament the Pool Dam part at least, while sanitation was still a problem in some areas. Pool Dam was eventually severed from the parish of Stoke and became part of Newcastle Union in February 1875. January 1875 brought an excessive number of applications for relief, mainly because of sickness such as influenza and bronchitis caused by the changeable weather. In the week ending 16th January there were 123 in the workhouse slightly less than the previous year but over 570 people had needed out door relief. The schoolmistress had resigned and was moving to Toxteth so a new schoolmistress would need to be appointed.

Bronchitis and pneumonia were still prevalent in March and there had been a fatal case of typhoid but every precaution had been taken to stop the spread of the disease.

A discussion about the increase of poverty was undertaken in June 1875 as the increase in poor relief had almost doubled over a period of fifteen years. However the population had also increased. Bronchitis, pneumonia and scarlet fever were still prevalent in June.

In September 1875 a return was prepared by Mr. Edwards, the workhouse master as to the religious persuasion of the inmates. This revealed fifty five adults and twenty eight children were in favour of the church of England, seven adults and one child were Wesleyan, five adults were New Connexion Methodist, two adults and one child were Primitive Methodist, and one adult Roman Catholics.

There was a severe epidemic of malignant measles in January 1876 and many children had died in the outlying villages of the parish. The weather was very severe so bronchitis was also prevalent and often fatal. It was decided at the Guardians meeting to improve the water supply at the workhouse. At another meeting the Guardians decided to find out how much it would cost to provide baths for vagrants as this would deter them from entering the workhouse.

A report in the Staffordshire Sentinel of 23 May 1877 notes that there are still no baths for vagrants but that the Guardians had looked at a separate 'cell' system used in the Stoke workhouse where the number of vagrants had decreased. The Guardians appointed a committee to deal with this matter. The report also stated that bronchitis and pneumonia were prevalent due to the easterly winds. If you look at the geography of the area you can see that Newcastle is more or less to the west of Stoke which produced a great deal of smoke from the pottery industry so bronchitis and pneumonia were inevitable.

By June 1877 the committee had visited several other

workhouses, Stoke, Stone and Stafford. In Stoke the tramps were put to stone breaking in exchange for accommodation. In Stone and Stafford they did oakum picking. It was suggested that each tramp be kept for three days and provided with work. It was thought that this would lessen the number of tramp paupers. The committee thought that stone breaking would be the best employment for tramps at the Newcastle workhouse and they recommended that a suitable building was erected and that baths be provided. Yet again it was decided to defer this until Chell workhouse had been visited.

In July 1877, a decision was reached and the Board of Guardians decided to erect a tramp ward on a site detached from the workhouse introducing a separate cell system. At the end of August, a report in the Staffordshire Sentinel shows that the decision had not really been made and there was much discussion over whether the new building should be detached or connected to the workhouse and after a vote, the subject of the tramps building would be reconsidered. This is a quote from the Staffordshire Sentinel of 19 September 1877; 'The Newcastle Guardians were equally divided on Monday upon the question whether or not a previous resolution respecting the site of the proposed new tramps ward should be reconsidered. Some Guardians reasonably objected to re-open a question which the Board had discussed and decided. Other Guardians urged, again with reason, that the previous decision had been hastily arrived at in opposition to the recommendation of a committee which had carefully considered the whole subject, and that, if acted upon, it would involve additional expenses both present and future. The Chairman, according to precedent, gave his casting vote so as to allow the Guardians another opportunity of considering the subject.'

The Staffordshire Sentinel of 28 September 1877 reported on the Guardians Meeting where the vagrant/tramp question was again discussed. Advice had been obtained from the Local Government Board and a decision was made on the plan inn favour of the wards would be attached to the workhouse. By early November the Local Government Board agreed to sanction the plans but offered suggestions for the Guardians to consider so a meeting between the Guardians and the Board was agreed. December brought another meeting and a proper plan was to be prepared. In 1878 the Staffordshire Sentinel of 5th April gave a brief summary of the meeting of the Board of Guardians stating that the number of vagrants had increased by no less than 891 over the previous year , a 'proof that vagrants considered the Newcastle workhouse an eligible place of entertainment'.

Over the next couple of years, all seemed satisfactory but a report in the Staffordshire Sentinel of 4 March 1880 gives an insight into how difficult life was for some families and how much they hated the workhouse. George Frederick Pover, a tailor was charged with neglecting to provide adequate food and clothing for his children. He had already been in prison because of this. Up to 10th February, George, his wife and children had been inmates of the Stoke workhouse and George had given notice to go out. George's wife was near her confinement and weak due to the previous neglect so they were advised not to leave, as she could die. George insisted in taking them out and later that evening George's wife called at a house in Newcastle asking for herself and her children to sit by the fire. She was allowed to do this but was taken ill and put to bed where she was confined early the next morning. George had asked for medical treatment from the Master of the workhouse and this was done for a week until George took her away from the house. George's wife and children were taken by the police to the Newcastle workhouse but left the following day being brought back again the following night, the newly born baby having died in the mothers arms. George was sent to prison for six months with hard labour. He stated that didn't want them to be in the workhouse eating 'a paupers loaf'.

Only the destitute and those unable to look after them selves could enter the workhouse. The relieving officer who dealt with those needing poor relief would obviously know when people had to enter the workhouse. According to the rules for the Newcastle workhouse paupers could only be admitted by one of the following ways;

a) by a written or printed order of the Board of Guardians signed by their clerk;
b) by a provisional order in writing signed by an overseer or relieving officer;
c) by the Master of the workhouse without any such order in case of any urgent or sudden necessity.

Once a person actually got inside the workhouse they would go to a separate room where they would be examined by the Medical officer. This examination would decide to which ward the person would go to. If they were ill they would go to the sick ward or to the ward for lunatics and idiots.

After the Medical examination, the person would then be thoroughly 'cleansed' and given the workhouse dress to wear, their own clothes being 'purified' and put into storage. The workhouse clothing may have been made in the workhouse by the inmates. The person who would by then have been classified (see previous) would then be assigned to the correct ward.

Admission registers contain basic information on those admitted, generally name, age, where born, religious preference, occupation if any, and maybe any observations such as infirmity or blindness. Sadly the admissions registers for the Newcastle workhouse are not available.

Once in the workhouse then those able bodied would be given work. Women and girls helped in the sick ward or in caring for the infants as well as household tasks such as making beds and laundry work. Everyday life was strict. Up at six in the morning with a roll call and inspection at six thirty followed by breakfast. Work began at seven with dinner at twelve noon then work again until six followed by supper and the end bed at eight. In the winter months everything was an hour later until lunch time then it was the same as the summer.

There were strict rules and orders in the workhouse. No-one could eat until grace had been said and could not leave either until after Grace. The house had to be kept clean and windows opened. No-one could leave without permission. Anyone stealing, drunk, swearing, quarrelling or fighting would be punished. Church or some other place of worship had to be attended on Sunday or miss a meal. Disobedience was also punished. There were other rules many punishable by missing a meal or even two meals. Theft and wilful damage could be punished by a JP in a court. Being drunk or rude or aggressive could be punished by being confined alone in a room for up to twelve hours. It was in fact like a prison and in some workhouse the inmates felt they were better looked after in prison than in the workhouse and deliberately did wrong so that they would go to prison.

The 1881 census shows that Thomas Edwards was still the Master of the Workhouse. He was aged thirty two but was already widowed In the census of 1871 he was living in Hall Street, Newcastle with his wife Elizabeth and was working as a solicitors clerk. Thomas had married Elizabeth Stanway in 1869 and she died in 1878 the same year as the birth of their son Thomas Henry. Thomas's parents were Thomas Edwards and Hannah Hodgkinson and the censuses show a Sarah Edwards born 1840, sister to Thomas. She is possibly the Sarah Edwards who is the Matron of the workhouse. Thomas has two children with him, Alice aged six and Thomas Henry aged two. Also on the staff are a schoolmistress, a nurse, a cook and a man working as both porter and baker. There were one hundred and fifty five inmates on the day of the census, thirty nine of these being children under eleven years of age.

In June 1882 the Staffordshire Advertiser reported on the Guardians meeting. One item of discussion was burials of those who died in the workhouse. Mistakes had been made in the past (not necessarily in Newcastle), paupers had been buried under the wrong name or in the wrong cemetery and on odd occasions there had been no body in the coffin. The Guardians were aware that great care must be taken over burials.

It could be thought that workhouse life had changed over the years and especially since the Local Government Board took over but it was still the Board of Guardians who controlled everything. There are many horrific stories of workhouse life but as far as I know no-one has written about life in the Newcastle workhouse so I can only deduce how it was from the reports of Guardians, Local Government Boards and those in newspapers.

The Guardians gave their chairman Mr. T. F. Twemlow, a dinner at the Borough Arms Hotel in Newcastle according to the Staffordshire Advertiser of 30 June 1883. They were provided with a 'sumptuous repast'. This was followed by many toasts, the whole report in the newspaper being almost a full column in length. I wonder if they spared a thought for those in the workhouse and in their care.

The Staffordshire Sentinel of 3rd May 1889 reports on the Annual General Meeting of the North Staffs branch of the Manchester School for the Deaf and Dumb. One of the children at the Manchester school, William Arrowsmith, had not been sent to the school again as the Newcastle Guardians had declined to maintain him during the holidays and considered they had not further responsibility for him.

But what of the inmates? I find groups of children, all one family, particularly tragic. There are three such children in the workhouse in 1881, Emma Edge born 1872, Mary Edge born 1870 and Ralph Edge born 1867. In 1871 they are living with their parents George and Emma at 4 Stafford Street, Newcastle. Emma died first in 1877 followed by George in 1880. Not only had the three children lost both their parents but the two girls would be separated from their brother in the workhouse. Another brother Thomas born in 1860 had died in 1874.

Another family, fairly unusual in that it consists of the father William Till, a widower aged fifty two and three of his children, George aged eight, Sarah aged nine and Henry aged eleven. In 1871, the family are living at 18 Goose Street, Newcastle. William and his wife Fanny have six children on this census; Annie, 17, Catherine 15, William 13, Eli 10, Fanny

6 and Sarah 1. Fanny, Williams wife, died in 1873. In 1881 the young Fanny was a boarder with a family in Stoke. Catherine had married and Eli was with the Mantle family in Leycett. William was working as a miner in Walsall and Annie may have married. Father William died in the workhouse in 1890. George married that year and moved to Walsall.

There were also two Grocott children in the workhouse in 1881. Alice was eleven years old and Samuel fourteen years old. In 1871 they were living with their parents George and Ann in Clayton. George had been born in Cheshire. Ann died in 1876 and it seems that George put the children in the workhouse then moved back to Cheshire where he died in 1907.

Another family worth a mention are Martha Newton aged 34 and widowed and her sons William aged eleven and George Henry. The father George had died in 1876 and Martha died in 1882, possibly in the workhouse. Both William and George Henry left the workhouse at some point and married in 1889 and 1911 respectively in Lancashire. These families show the different sets of circumstances that can lead to living in the workhouse.

In December 1890 there was a fire in the workhouse. Six people died either due to suffocation from the smoke or from injuries from falling debris. The women's wing where the fire broke out was two storied. The fire was first noticed just after 6 a.m. by an old lady who shared a separate bedroom and sitting room with three others. She raised the alarm and many inmates were able to escape. The fire and the following inquest were reported in not only the local newspapers but in others nationwide. A comment was made in the Derby Mercury that there was a lack of available water apart from a hand pump and that a chain of men had carried buckets of water to douse the fire. Those who died were Lucy Smith, 69, a widow; Martha Smith, 75, a widow; Margaret Conway, 73, single; Sarah Meakin, 32, Single; Annie Burrows, 29, single; and William Wood aged 3. Both of the last two were orphans.

After the fire which had burnt down the two storey female wing, the building had to be rebuilt. After the inquest where the questioning was deep, it was obvious that changes had to be made. As the fire had made the national news then other workhouses looked at their premises and what kind of changes needed to be made especially where water supplies and escape routes were concerned.

The Stoke Board of Guardians had offered to board, clothe and educate children from the Newcastle Workhouse for the sum of four shillings per week per child. Thirty three girls were moved to take up this offer. Estimates for the cost of rebuilding were made and insurance claims made enabling rebuilding to go ahead. By 14th February 1891 plans for the rebuilding were waiting for the approval of the Local Government Board. The new structure would be fireproof with iron girders and concrete floors. The ceilings in the current buildings were to be made fireproof and better facilities for escape from fire were to be included.

Chapter 7

In the Guardians Minutes during this and the following years it is noted that gifts of papers and periodicals were given for the use of the inmates. Occasionally there were also gifts of books.

The minutes of the Guardians meeting on 25 April 1891 noted the length of service of some of the Guardians. William Mellard for example had been a Guardian for twenty four years. Also noted was that the workhouse pump had to be repaired at a cost of £15 17s 6d – a large sum of money then.

The Staffordshire Advertiser of 19 September 1891 reported on the official returns showing the cost of pauperism in Staffordshire. Newcastle had spent £1045 in maintenance and £906 in out-relief. This was for half a year. Another official return stated accommodation for the sick in Staffordshire. At the Newcastle workhouse there were fifty eight beds in the sick wards. In September the previous year, there were fifty eight patients, fifty four in October and fifty six in November. There was one paid nurse at that time.

In May 1892, the Guardians had decided to borrow £9000 over thirty years and £1973 over fifteen years, to finance the rebuilding of the wing destroyed in the fire. This is eighteen months after the fire. Bureaucracy moved slowly even then.

In September 1894, a revised dietary table was put in place. This afforded more variety at the same cost but additional work in the kitchen. On Sunday a hot meat and potato dinner replace the rice and treacle. In this month there had also been a gift of old books from the Free Library and illustrated papers from the railway bookstall.

February 1895 brought vagrancy to the fore again. The Board of Guardians recommended a system of uniformity of diet, type of work and accommodation, some method of identification of men really in search of work and repression as far as possible of women habitually wandering about with children. It was noted that there was not enough accommodation in the Newcastle workhouse for vagrants to stay two nights so a decision had to be postponed until after a County meeting on vagrancy.

Going back to 1891 and the census taken a few months after the fire, there were 146 inmates and of these 89 were males and 34 were children aged ten and under. There were three families on this census that I found interesting. The first of these is Thomas Paton, 34, married, his wife Jane, 30 (born in Ireland) and their two children Joseph aged 12 and John aged 1. In 1881 they are living in Roebuck Lane, Newcastle with Margaret aged five and Joseph aged two. Thomas was a general labourer but somehow their lives had changed for the worse and they ended up in the workhouse apart from Margaret. Thomas died that year in the last quarter of the year so may have been ill before that and unable to work and Jane may not have been able to work because of the age of the youngest child. In 1901 though Jane and John are still in the workhouse but by 1911 John is working as a miner and boarding with a family.

The second family consisted of four children John Taplin, aged thirteen, Florence Taplin aged seven, George Taplin aged five and Charles Taplin also aged five. In 1881 the family was in Pump Street with George their father and Jane their mother. There were other children Thomas than aged seven, Sarah A aged five and Jane aged one. The mother Jane had died in 1888 and in 1891 George their father was in prison. (In 1901 and 1911 George was in the workhouse) The young Jane had been adopted by Samuel and Eliza Mellor and was with them in 1891. In 1901 George and Charles were both working as brick pressers and lodging with the same family. Florence was with relatives in Manchester and John had married and was living with his in-laws.

The third family consisted of Mary Appleby aged 46 and widowed and her two children Albert aged ten and George aged eight. In 1881 Mary was living with her husband Charles, a master boot maker, in Shraley Brook, Halmerend. There were several other children in 1881. Isabella, then aged ten was a domestic servant in Swynnerton in 1891; Margaret Elizabeth then aged eight was married in 1890; Emma Jane then aged seven; Richard aged five, who in 1891 was an agricultural servant at a farm in Audley; Thomas W aged three and Albert aged one. Charles had died in 1882 aged only thirty six. But somehow between 1891 and 1901 Mary had left the workhouse. In 1901 she can be found at 71 Garner Street, Stoke with Emma J, John and George. In 1911 she is at 22 Campbell Terrace. Hanley with John and George who are both working on haulage in the mine. Mary states that she had ten children one of whom had died. This family show there is life after the workhouse and it also shows the children looking after their mother.

So did the start of the 1900s bring more changes in the workhouse or was life still as hard as ever for the poorer paid labourers and servants?

At the start of 1900 there were 259 inmates in the workhouse and the beds in the workhouse hospital were fully occupied, the number of chronic cases increasing. In March 1900 an inspection of the workhouse stated that all was in order and the sick and infirm appeared comfortable and well cared for. A Government inspector visited the workhouse in April 1900 and commented on the school. Singing was very good, but reading needed a 'more spirited' approach while arithmetic was weak in Standard V.

The yearly Lady Day report on vagrants stated that 5,399 vagrants had passed through the workhouse during the year.

Chapter 8

1901 brought changes to the diet again. These were because too much bread was wasted and the diet was monotonous. The diet would now be more varied within the choices given by the Board. In September 1901 a tender was put out for iron staircases and building alterations. These were possibly to do with fire prevention and escape.

In the 1901 census there were 224 inmates in the workhouse. Thirty one of these were children of ten and under. Mr. Thomas Edwards was still the Master and his wife the Matron. His son John now thirteen and daughter Annie now nine are also living with them. There are now more nurses, a superintendent nurse and four other nurses. There is also a laundress and an industrial trainer. Women industrial trainers taught the girls sewing, knitting, straw plaiting and other skills. Male industrial trainers taught the boys skill in leather work and carpentry.

There were two families that interested me on the 1901 census. The first of these was Hannah Keen age 44 and widowed who was in the workhouse with her two children Sidney aged eight and Fanny aged three. In 1891 Hannah and her husband Samuel are living at 5 Garden Street, Newcastle with some of their children, Rebecca, 15 (who married Isaac Pepper in 1896), Samuel 11, Walter 8, and John T aged 5. Next door at 7 Garden Street was Rebecca Keen aged 72 and widowed with her granddaughter Mary Ann (who married in 1898). In 1901 Samuel is a boarder at 26 Bow Street, Walter is with Rebecca and her husband Isaac and John is a boarder in Castle Street, Newcastle.. Hannah's husband had died in 1896 leaving her and two of the children in the workhouse. By 1911 Sidney is living with Rebecca and Isaac, I do not know what happened to Fanny but Hannah is still in the workhouse in 1911.

The other family is Jane Bennett aged 45 and widowed who is with her son James in the workhouse. Jane married Abraham Bennett after his first wife died and they can be found on the 1891 census at 9 May Street, Newcastle. There are several children, Abraham 26 (obviously from the first marriage), Albert 12, George 10, Joseph 7, Samuel 4 and Jim or James aged one. Abraham senior died later in 1891. The younger Abraham is married and Joseph and Samuel are boarders elsewhere in 1901. I cannot find Albert or George in 1901 although George married Emily Bennett in 1901. In 1911 Jim is living with George and Emily. I cannot find Jane in 1911 or a death registration.

One of the things I have found out about people in the workhouse is that they can just disappear. I have often wondered during this research if people gave their real names or an assumed name to avoid detection perhaps from crime or violent partners.

In November 1902, the problem of children left in the workhouse by their mothers was discussed. The mothers were vagrants and it was difficult to get them to provide for their children who had to be maintained by the workhouse. Two mothers had done this recently then moved away. After 1900 many documents held in archives and other places were destroyed during the war. This means that newspaper reports and a few other records are those available. It is difficult to put together a coherent picture of what was going on during the next thirty years as Guardians minutes do not give the details often needed.

The Staffordshire Advertiser of 7 May 1904 gives a long report on the Guardians meeting. Details of vagrant numbers are given for three years. These are divided into men, women and children but are difficult to read. There seems to be around 6 – 7000 vagrants per year using the workhouse with several hundred of these being children. This was a big concern but no way of dealing with the children was put forward. Another cause for concern was the use of the workhouse by lodging house keepers who sent an ill lodger to the workhouse instead of to the hospital. The committee felt that there were too many lodging house in the town. The ladies on the committee were to visit the workhouse to see the children and to see whether it was better to board them out or use the scattered homes system. They would report back later.

Later in May that year, another lengthy report appeared in the Staffordshire Advertiser. Ten people from the workhouse had been moved to the smallpox hospital at Bagnall, not because they had the disease but to isolate them as they had been in contact with someone who had. It was recommended that the vagrants ward be closed and no cases of sickness be admitted to the workhouse hospital. The Inspector said that closing the vagrants ward was not the answer as they would then go into lodging houses and spread the disease even more. The tramps in the vagrancy ward could be vaccinated if they were willing. This was agreed. More discussion followed about finding work for vagrants maybe sending them to labour camps.

The 27th August 1904 brought reports of another fire at the workhouse. The fire had started in the early hours of Sunday morning about 1.30 am. It was discovered by Miss E Langley, the laundress who woke to find smoke in her second floor room which was directly over the store room. She made her way out and across the landing to the womens room where there were fifty women and about a dozen young children. These left the building via the outside iron staircase. Miss Langley then woke the Master and other staff members who used a hosepipe to put out the fire. The main seat of the fire was in a cupboard in the store room. The ceiling was fireproof and this had stopped the fire from spreading. The cause of the fire was the spontaneous combustion of matches kept in the cupboard. Fire drills were held regularly and this had helped to deal with the fire. The Guardians made a decision to use safety matches in the future and to possibly employ a night watchman.

Later in the year, vagrants caused more problems as there were too many of them and not enough accommodation. It was easier for them to come to Newcastle rather than Stoke where the vagrant wards were empty. There is little documentation for the next few years but changes were on the way. Old age pensions introduced by Lloyd George in 1909 helped to alleviate the dear of entering the workhouse.

Chapter 9

Some time between 1901 and 1911, possibly around 1906 after the death of Mr Edwards, a new Master was appointed, Mr Herbert Bratt and his wife Emma Elizabeth became Matron. Previously they had both worked in the workhouse at Bloxwich

The Staffordshire Sentinel of 3rd January 1911 has a long report with the title 'Children's Day at the Workhouse', and subtitled 'Christmas Tree Festival'. The Matron Mrs. Bratt and other lady members of staff had decorated the schoolroom making it bright and attractive. Evergreens had been draped on the top of the walls and also festooned from the corners of the room to the centre. There was a huge Christmas tree and many presents situated in an alcove. Guests from town had been invited including some of the Guardians. The children presented a musical programme performing action songs, some songs in harmony and some solo songs. Then presents from the tree were distributed by Mrs Bratt and two of the nurses. Each girl received a daintily dressed doll and a large box of chocolates while the boys received a mechanical toy, drums, magic lanterns and a box of sweetmeats. Even the babies had a present being given a rattle. All the children also received an apple, an orange and a miniature teapot or jug filled with sweets. A vote of thanks at the end was given by the Rev. P.E. Mainwaring who said that he and his fellow guardians had tried to do everything they could to brighten the life of the children entrusted to their care.

I see this report as a sign of great change in the way the children were treated in the workhouse.

A couple of days later the Staffordshire Sentinel reported on the 'workhouse and old-age pensions'. I quote 'The present week is witnessing a mild exodus of old people from our workhouses. With the New Year the provision in the Old Age Pension Act for the removal of pauper disqualification has come into operation and tomorrow many old people, who have hitherto been debarred from enjoying the State Pension will draw 5 shillings from the Post Office'. Although this meant that many older people could leave the workhouse and become independent, there were many who could not do so because of physical or mental infirmity. Many would prefer to stay in the workhouse where their needs were met than try to live independently on five shillings per week. The Master of the Newcastle workhouse thought that those who could not live with relatives so went into lodging houses might miss the company of the friends they had made in the workhouse and they would also find it difficult to live on such a small amount of money after paying for their lodgings.

At a Guardians meeting later in January there was a heated discussion about the amount paid to maintain a person in Northwich workhouse who had asked for four shillings per week. The Newcastle Guardians offered to pay three shillings and sixpence at which point, one member stated that this board was one of the meanest in the country so four shillings was then agreed.

In April 1911 the workhouse was given a piano and the Guardians agreed to pay for it to be tuned three times every year. So now we come to the 1911 census, the last census available at the time of writing, before the workhouse was closed down in the early 1930s. As mentioned earlier the Master is Herbert Bratt and his wife Emma Elizabeth is the

Matron. The workhouse now has a proper infirmary with five nurses in total. There is a Superintendent nurse, a staff nurse and three other nurses. There is also an assistant matron, a girls industrial trainer, a laundress, a cook, a labour master, a boys industrial trainer and a housemaid.

The housemaid Clara Flackett is in my family tree. Her father William Henry Flackett was my great great grandfathers brother. William Henry was born in 1834 to Thomas Flackett and Prudence Blood. He married Patricia Leabond but they soon separated and William Henry can be found living in Armitage with a housekeeper Catherine Conway and several children with the surname Conway, one of these being Clara. After the death of either Patience or William Henry the children all changed their surname to Flackett.

There were 206 inmates in 1911, 118 males and 88 females. There were 34 children aged twelve and under. There are several interesting inmates at this time. One of these is Sarah Jane Beardmore, aged 37 and married, and her daughter Annie aged ten. In 1901 Sarah Ann and her husband Frederick are living in Newcastle with three children, Harriet aged five, Frederick aged three and Sarah Ann aged four months (I assume this is the Annie in the workhouse) In 1911 Sarah Jane states that she is married had been married for fifteen years, that she gave birth to four children one of whom had died. So where is her husband? He can be found as a prisoner in Stafford Gaol in 1911.

Another family consists of Jane Ratcliffe, aged 31 and married for nineteen years with three children, James aged eleven, Kenneth aged seven and Willie aged four. She had borne six children of whom two had died. In 1901 she and James and a son called Herbert are boarders at 2 Back Holborn. And that is where this trail stops. I can find no other information about this family at the time of writing.

The next family consists of Mary Tomlinson aged thirty seven and married for sixteen years, and her four children John aged ten, Alfred aged eight, Willie aged five and Annie aged one, all born in Audley. Mary had married Alfred Tomlinson in 1896. She states that she had ten children of whom five had died. In 1911 Alfred is living with his married sister in Butt Lane. Had Mary and Alfred separated and if so why?

Another married woman with children is also in the workhouse in 1911. She is Sarah Ann Brassington aged thirty eight and who had been married for nineteen years. She had born eight children of whom one had died. With her in the workhouse are Rose aged eleven, Albert Henry aged nine, Charles William aged eight and Nellie aged six. In 1901 Sarah Ann and her husband John are living at Cracow Moor, Betley. The other children are with them, Arthur aged seven, Bertha M aged six, Nellie aged four (I think this may be the child who died and the later Nellie named after her), John T aged three and Rose aged two. In 1911 Arthur is working as a farm labourer in Madeley and Bertha M is an inmate at the Sisters of Mercy in South Manchester. Sarah states she is married but I cannot find her husband in 1911 neither can I find a death registration.

My final story is quite sad. Caroline Pemberton aged thirty two and single is in the workhouse with three children, Elizabeth aged ten, Ernest aged four, and Amos aged one. In 1901 Caroline known as Carrie and Elizabeth aged six months are boarding at No 1 Court, Holborn, Newcastle. Carrie is working as a charwoman. In 1891 Caroline aged fourteen and her sister

Mary aged ten are in the Spittall workhouse in Stoke. Caroline died in 1915, Amos in 1922 but Ernest lived much long into his old age.

One of things I notice about the 1911 census was the different occupations of the inmates. There were quite a few ironworkers, a chair bottom repairer, an umbrella maker, a traction engine driver, several tailors and coal workers. What could be called fairly skilled occupations did not mean you lived a better life. You could still be poor and not be able to support yourself or your family.

There are many changes to come in the future, National Insurance Acts, proposals for separating mentally ill people in the workhouse and the boarding out of children. There doesn't seem to be a schoolmistress or schoolmaster in the 1911 census but that doesn't mean there wasn't one. But if the children were boarded out then they would go to the local school.

In February of 1911, the Guardians were faced with an unusual situation. An application for relief had been received by an old soldier who was aged sixty eight. While serving in Canada he had married a Canadian woman but when they returned to England she didn't like it and went back to Canada. The old soldier had been living with a woman for nearly forty years. The woman was receiving the old age pension but he needed help. The main question was if it was legal to give the old soldier help. It was possible that his wife had died. The matter was adjourned until the next meeting. When the Relieving Officer stated that he had arranged a civil marriage for the old soldier and the woman he had been living with. Once this marriage had occurred the old soldier was able to receive some help and was given two shillings per week and one loaf of bread.

The newspapers often bring little snippets to light about events in the workhouse which do not make the Guardians minutes. In June 1911 a vagrant who refused to perform his allotted task of stone breaking was sent to prison for one month. In January 1912, another vagrant tore his clothes and asked for better ones. He was sent to prison for twenty one days. In the same newspaper is a report of an attempted suicide by a depressed man. He was sent to the workhouse Infirmary for a week to help him to recover. In the same month a father who had deserted his four children and left them with his mother who could not cope and put them in the workhouse, was sent to prison for one month.

In late 1911 there had been a Boarding Out Order and this was discussed by the Guardians at one of their meetings in January 1912. The Guardians were not clear about the medical treatment for any boarded out children who became ill. This was clarified by the Local Government Board and seemed to satisfy the Guardians. There were strict rules for the boarding out of children from the workhouse. Every child had to be visited periodically by a woman officer, children should not be boarded out in any home where the foster mother was frequently absent, homes with male lodgers were to be avoided and the child should have suitable clothes and an allowance for their repair and renewal available to the foster parents.

In 1911 Winston Churchill had spoken of the need to separate those with mental illness into camps where they could work. A bill was eventually passed in 1913 but the Guardians had already been discussing this in 1912. They felt that maybe they should combine with other Union workhouses to provide separate accommodation, often known as colonies, for the treatment of the feeble minded and epileptic. At the current time the total cost of lunatics was 15s 2d per head per week. There was much discussion and many suggestions such as removing all the children and using that accommodation for the lunacy cases. This was agreed but then the decision was deferred until the next meeting so they could think about it more.

In April 1912 there was a miners strike. Some miners belonged to a Union but others did not. Miners in the Union were not allowed to receive poor relief. The other miners who had requested such relief were thought to sympathise with the Union miners so the Guardians refused their request. When the topic of the colony for lunatics arose at this meeting, the Guardians were told that unless the children were all boarded out then a grant for a separate colony of lunatics would not be given.

Also this time there had been a request for the workhouse staff to decide whether they wanted to opt in or out of the new National Insurance scheme. Most of the staff decided to opt out. This was a new scheme which provided sickness benefit and unemployment benefit for some short time but the staff at the workhouse thought they were well looked after where sickness was concerned.

The most interesting report of 1913, for me at least, is that of the death of Annie Stubbs, a single woman aged twenty eight with two children. She had gone to the workhouse where she became ill with severe pains and a blue-black line around her gums which was associated with lead poisoning. She died on 11 December 1913 at the workhouse having previously lived in

Merrial Street. The post mortem showed lead poisoning and that she had been pregnant recently but was not pregnant at the time of death. She was believed to have taken a preparation containing lead for an unlawful purpose which brought on convulsions and caused death.

But back to the Mental Deficiency Act of 1913. This Act established the Board of Control for Lunacy and Mental Deficiency to oversee the implementation of the provisions for lunacy and mental deficiency. There were four classes of people defined;
a) idiots – those who were unable to guard themselves from common physical dangers;
b) imbeciles – not as bad as idiots but who could not manage themselves;
c) feeble minded persons – who needed supervision or some form of control for their own protection or for the protection of others;
d) moral imbeciles – mentally weak but who were vicious or of criminal tendencies and where punishment had not effect.

This Act remained in force until 1959 when it was repealed.

In January 1914, Dr. Menzies from the Cheddleton Asylum was appointed as a Consultant Medical Officer for three months to assist in the treatment of chargeable epileptics and the feeble minded. The Guardians although accepting this had mixed feelings about it. They had other things to deal with such as the possible closure of the tramp ward. Meanwhile the Stoke Board of Guardians had set up cottage homes for their workhouse children and had accommodated 220 children this way.

The Poor Law Institution Order of 1913 was causing problems in Newcastle workhouse because of the vagrant children. There needed to be some kind of receiving home for them so it was decided to build one. The average number of children was fifteen so it would not have to be a large building.

The Guardians also decided that a rota should be set up for visiting the workhouse just before the fortnightly meetings. This had been done before but some members did not visit and ignored the rota. The Guardians of the Stoke workhouse had offered to take in the Newcastle vagrants or casuals as they were now called, for a payment of £52 per annum. This was considered too expensive so an offer was to be made based on the cost of the past year.

In March, the Staffordshire Advertiser reported on a meeting of the National Union of Women Workers. It was noted that there were many feeble minded women in the maternity wards of workhouses and that these women needed to be in places or homes where they would be able to do some kind of work. May, 1914 brought the Annual Meeting of the Guardians. It was decided to hand over the care of the casuals to Stoke workhouse and to erect a separate building as a home for the remaining children.

A male inmate who was helpless due to a broken spine had been upsetting the nursing staff with bad language and name calling. It was decided to ask Stoke workhouse to take him as they had a male nurse. The month of May also brought the feeble minded back into focus. The Staffordshire Joint Poor Law committee had decided to purchase Low Hill estate at Bushbury near Wolverhampton as a colony for the feeble minded. The state was 170 acres in size, had a mansion, a cottage, a lodge and several outbuildings. It would cost £11,500 to purchase. There was a total of two hundred cases in Staffordshire who need to be sent to a colony.

The Guardians were looking at the purchase of land adjoining the Newcastle workhouse for the purpose of erecting a children's home as at the end of the year it would be compulsory to provide accommodation for the 'ins and outs', mainly the vagrant children.

In September the Staffordshire Joint Poor Law committee agreed to negotiate the taking over of surplus accommodation in various workhouses, including Newcastle, for feeble minded cases.

The Local Government Board issued a new order which came into force on 31 October concerning the diet and other rules concerning the casuals. Now the casuals had to receive a midday meal at the workhouse or a wayside station or be given food to take with them.

Accommodation which had been offered to the Staffordshire Joint Poor Law in September now came with specific requests in November. Not only was there to be accommodation for the feeble minded but workshops needed to be erected, extra land provided and special staff employed. The Guardians suggested a charge of 11shillings or 11 shillings and 6 pence per head per week for that. A programme for the workshop activities needed to be prepared as well. Such activities could be tailoring, mat and brush making for the men and bookbinding for the women.

In January 1915 the Mental Deficiency Committee asked the Guardians to let them know of cases of mental deficiency which would benefit from being in a mental ward or in the workhouse whether or not they were a pauper. Later in March 1915, the Local Government Board directed that all children should be removed from the precincts of the workhouse. Land had been secured for the erection of a children's home in Thistleberry Avenue and tenders had been received, the successful firm being asked to employ local labour as much as possible.

Stoke Guardians had also enquired if Newcastle could provide accommodation for some of their inmates who might have to move out if accommodation was needed by the War Office at Stoke workhouse. The Newcastle Guardians agreed to take fifty aged and infirm men and fifty aged and infirm women.

At the beginning of April 1915, the Local Government Board said they were unable to authorise expenditure for the building of the children's home so this scheme was put in abeyance. The old schoolroom in the workhouse could be utilised for girls and the Stoke Guardians would be asked if they could take the boys. Stoke Guardians had also requested more money for the vagrants they had taken in for Newcastle as the number had increased. A sum of £60 per annum was agreed.

Vagrants had been registered at workhouses using a case card scheme and this had helped with a reduction in begging on the streets and had also stopped loitering by beggars in isolated places. It had been noted that in general, casuals travelled from one ward to another.

By May 1915, the Newcastle children had been taken in the Stoke Cottage Homes and there was an agreement for Stoke inmates to come to Newcastle to make room for wounded soldiers. Meat had become scarce and so the diet in the workhouse would be amended to use less meat but the nutrition value was to stay the same.

An interesting case regarding two children came before the Guardians meeting in October 1915. Two young boys had been born in Germany to an English mother and a German father. The father had deserted them and the mother had died and they were now in the workhouse.. The Guardians had tried to board them out but no one would take them because they were German. The Guardians wondered if it would be possible to deport them to Germany. (in the middle of a war with Germany!)

More inmates were coming from the Stoke workhouse to stay in Newcastle as more accommodation was needed for wounded soldiers. This meant there was a total of seventy men and fifty nine women from Stoke in the Newcastle workhouse. There now eleven Newcastle children in the Stoke Cottage Homes.

1916 brought in new child welfare schemes. The Guardians of the workhouse also dealt with out relief for those who needed help so any welfare changes for children also involved the Guardians. Because of the large number of baby and infant deaths, a health visiting scheme was being put in place. Staffordshire County Council were proud of being one of the most progressive councils in the country and hoped that this scheme would get going thereby saving lives.

As the war progressed there was a warning of air raids and by February 1916, the windows in the workhouse had been darkened. The workhouse was also looking for a labour master, a strong, active, single man or widower who was ineligible for the Army.

Another scheme came in during 1917 for the treatment of venereal diseases. The treatment was free to all and given at the North Staffordshire Infirmary at Hartshill. The Newcastle Guardians agreed to join this scheme.

At the 1917 Annual Meeting of the Guardians, there were allegations of improper burials in that the deceased had been naked and laid on a bed of sawdust in the coffin. This was strongly denied by the workhouse Master and other members of his staff and the matter was dropped.

1917 was the year that the number of vagrants dropped greatly so there was unused accommodation. There were also suggestions that those vagrants still on the road should be made to settle. As the Newcastle vagrants stayed at the Stoke workhouse this could mean an increase in cost to Newcastle but it was decided to try it for twelve months (By February 1918, there were even less vagrants reported)

Christmas Day at the Newcastle workhouse was a happy but quiet day, the men receiving a gift of tobacco and the women a gift of fruit.

I have found very little about the workhouse for the next couple of years. In Newcastle, there were no children and no vagrants and possibly no inmates with mental illnesses either. Also the idea that the workhouse was for the poor and infirm was no longer seen in the same way.

Mr. Bratt was still the Master of the workhouse in 1919 as seen from a report of the Christmas festivities in the workhouse in the Staffordshire Advertiser of 3 January 1920. Those inmates who had no relatives or friends received a present. The men received extra tobacco and the women tea and sugar.

Towards the end of 1922, an attempted murder charge was reported in the Staffordshire Advertiser of 27 November and 4 December. Agnes Thomas aged 33 of Market Lane was charged with attempting to murder her daughter. They had been found on the canal bank wet through. A letter was found on Agnes which stated she was unhappy with something her husband had done. She was found to be suffering from a certain disease which had preyed on her mind. She had spent time first in the Stoke workhouse then the Newcastle workhouse until the case came to court. She was not convicted and the case was dismissed. Her husband assured the magistrates that he would look after his wife.

In January 1921 there was a proposal that the Newcastle Guardians would treat private patients in their hospital erecting an operating theatre and enlarging the mortuary. It was agreed to put these proposals to the Ministry of Health. There were many unemployed in 1921 although the stoppage by the miners was over so by September it was decided to continue to help, those unemployed and in distress, although the money would have to be paid back in some way.

The Staffordshire Advertiser of 19 April 1922 reported on the Newcastle Guardians meeting. There were several comments of note. The first was that the current Minister of Health was much more sympathetic to the Guardians than his predecessor and he had promised to support them in their work. A statement was made at the Poor Law Conference in February 1922 that the Boards of Guardians had been 'largely instrumental in saving the country from revolution'.

The Staffordshire Joint Vagrancy committee approved what was called the Yorkshire Scheme for treating vagrants who were aged or infirm. These vagrants were persuaded to enter a Poor Law Institution (the workhouse) and remain there as ordinary inmates. Their maintenance would be paid by the County Vagrancy committee. This was one way to take the vagrants off the roads. Ex-servicemen who were admitted to the casual wards were excused labour tasks but it had been found that many ex-servicemen had been vagrants before the war.

Christmas Day in the workhouse was reported as on a usual generous scale and everything was done to make it memorable and enjoyable. (Staffordshire Advertiser 6 January 1923). In July 1923, the Newcastle Guardians had a special meeting to discuss a labour test for the work shy. This test would be for applicants for unemployment relief. The labour tests would consist of stone breaking, wood sawing and chopping, pumping, gardening and other similar work. The men would work for eight hours each day for five days. They would receive five shillings, plus ten shillings for a wife and one shilling for each child. And also a four pound loaf for each woman and child. This was approved.

By 1924 there had been several threats to abolish the Board of Guardians but they were still doing their work and had been told they would continue to do so for at least another two years.

Another murder case appeared in December 1924. Mary Adeline Yeoman, a single woman aged twenty three was charged with the murder of her young son. She had been in the

Newcastle workhouse with her son and had then left taking the boy with her. Several hours later she appeared at her brothers without the boy who she said she had left either in or near the water. The body of the child was found in two feet of water at the Mill Bank Pool and she was later committed for trial at the Assizes.

The Vagrancy theme came to the fore again in 1929 where the future of the Staffordshire Joint Vagrancy committee was discussed, with a possible combining with other areas. The diet of the vagrants was also discussed and some thought that you could not expect the heavy work tasks to be done on such a poor diet. No changes were made despite this discussion.

In February 1930 the next to last meeting of the Guardians occurred. On April 1st their duties would be taken over by the county council. The workhouse closed in 1938.

Postcript

It has been an interesting study with many problems because of the lack of documentation. Some papers have been lost and others such as newspaper reports are so faint they cannot be read. I am still looking for information from 1930 to 1939 but having little success and I am also looking for photos.

The Newcastle workhouse in the process of demolition 1938 from the Warrillow Collection, Keele University Library. Photo by E J D Warrillow

Printed in Great Britain
by Amazon